Century Farm

poems by

Jessi Peterson

Finishing Line Press
Georgetown, Kentucky

Century Farm

Copyright © 2020 by Jessi Peterson
ISBN 978-1-64662-277-1 First Edition
All rights reserved under International and Pan-American Copyright Conventions. No part of this book may be reproduced in any manner whatsoever without written permission from the publisher, except in the case of brief quotations embodied in critical articles and reviews.

ACKNOWLEDGMENTS

Poems in this collection have appeared in the following publications:

NOTA—"Possum Lights", "Carp Quake"
Wisconsin People and Ideas—"Century Farm", "Sand County"
Wisconsin Poet's Calendar—"Pear Blossom", "Buzz Cut", "West with The Night"
Volume One—"The Dark Season"; "West with the Night"; "Looking Glass Prairie"
Twig—"Ashes and Fat"
Sky Island Journal (online journal)—"Irruption"
Crab Orchard Review (online journal)—"Songs My Mother Taught Me"
The Green Light Literary Journal (online journal)—"Hummingbird"

Publisher: Leah Maines
Editor: Christen Kincaid
Cover Art: Public Domain
Author Photo: Brandi Smith, Brandi Smith Photography
Cover Design: Elizabeth Maines McCleavy

Order online: www.finishinglinepress.com
also available on amazon.com

Author inquiries and mail orders:
Finishing Line Press
P. O. Box 1626
Georgetown, Kentucky 40324
U. S. A.

Table of Contents

Sand County 1

Lilac Time 2

Bloodroots 3

Pear Blossom 4

Hummingbird 5

Buzz Cut 6

Looking Glass Prairie 7

Roadkill 8

Summer Quilt 9

Carp Quake 10

Songs My Mother Taught Me 11

Late Harvest 12

Possum Lights 13

Ashes and Fat 14

The Dark Season 15

West with the Night 16

Frugality 17

Irruption 18

Epiphany 19

Noticing 20

Century Farm 21

Sand County

We trudge through last year's corn stubble in a wayward,
straggling line, drunken with the hour and the cold.
It's April, 4 AM, the air metallic in our noses.
We stoop low, clamber awkwardly into plywood boxes slouching
in slush, six strangers crammed together on a rough grainy bench.
We sit in silence, slurping coffee or inhaling its steam,
ears straining. There's a guy who doesn't get it two blinds over,
nattering on in the face of shushing. To block him from my mind,
I try to remember poems I memorized in fourth grade, one each week.
The roads in a yellow wood, the fog with cat feet, the wild geese
told to go. But I stop when I get to the one about the prairie.
You know, clover and a bee.
And reverie, broken now by a series of eerie, otherworldly
humming whoops. The talker two doors down shuts up
and we gingerly open the viewing hatches.
Dawn has crept out across the winter matted grass and one by one
the prairie chickens we have come to see venture into the open,
each male claiming a little circle of grace to stomp around on,
orange air sacks ballooning beneath his chin, a spiky feather crest
rearing up behind his head. They dance alone,
each angling for the best spot, booming
their bizarre, buzzing love call endlessly.
We all wait for the girl who never comes, not this morning at any rate.
A harrier swoops over on silent gray wings, breaks the undulating
spell of sound, sends the chickens into the tall grass like scattershot.
We stumble out of our blinds and back across the field to cold cars.
I warm my fingers, numb from gripping binoculars, against the heater.
I decide that Emily Dickinson didn't know dickcissel about the prairie.
How could she, cloistered in a white Amherst saltbox
where arching chestnuts and elms framed her world?
Here in the sand counties there is no frame,
just a bending ocean of grass under a skim milk sky.

Lilac Time

Consider the lilies, and the lilacs, all that's left of a cut-over farm.

Once a cathedral of white pine, until they cut and floated south
the forest that built the west, left behind a desert of stumps.
In what surely must be fertile soil, to grow trees of such stature.
Clear those stumps, you could grow cabbages
the size of hogshead casks, corn as high as heaven.

And they did, the Swedes, Germans, Poles, the men burning
and blasting, beating back the wild, panning the glacial till
for crops of gold. Their wives planted home, and hope, clutched
the idea of it close under winter's blanket.

Undone now, all that work—the draft horses lunging wetly
into their harnesses, tails swishing against the blackflies,
the endless shoveling, the dynamite.
Scraggly jack pine, spruce and tamarack have taken it all back, although

in May a chance drift of lilac, a memory of hope floats
low over the bog, whispering the secret those women
nearly knew: almost anything can be borne until lilac time.

Bloodroots

From late June's profusion of flowers
I should have picked the tiny lipstick-kiss pinks
balanced on slender, swaying stalks
or the white tower of pokeberry blossom,
always threatening to thread a poisonous path
between the pig-pen slats. I could have
chosen the gentians, nodding in deep blue dreams
under bumblebee buzz at the edge of the stream
or the purple candelabra of vervain that smelt acrid,
comforting even, like patent medicine that might work.

Instead I brought home a bouquet of baby bunnies,
eyes still closed, spilling softly over my clasped fingers
like wilting bloodroots, so fragile and quick to spoil.

Pear Blossom

The wind is ripe with rain.
The pear trees are in bloom,
tall, willowy girls wading through
the meadow's lush green waves,
skirts held high, blossoms full of
frothy salty sweet tang,
an inland sea welling up
from the soft dark earth.

Come September the tide will be out,
each pear a tidepool of sweet
juice, a sharp grit of sand in the teeth.

Hummingbird

The tiger brings her trophy, proud,
cannot understand my reprimand, nor that
I take the tiny bundle from her, walk out
into the bee loud summer clover to weep.
The finest jeweled avian scrap, so newly dead
I take one breath of hope, but then the tiny
neck lolls obscenely against my hand, free of intent,
smearing sweetness from its needle thin beak. One way,
a collar greenly black as the jungle night, the other a sharp,
metallic crimson, brighter than blood. I think then of
a painting by Sargent, Ellen Terry in her green beetle wing dress,
a thousand iridescent wings clasped as shields
against the warp and weft of wool,
soft chain mail for Lady Macbeth
with so much beauty and death in her hands,
and now in mine.

Buzz Cut

The bumbling mower lurches and weaves
over the scalp of the hill, mapping its phrenology of dirt,
drought and gophers. Back and forth
from brow to nape, shearing a full head
of alfalfa down to stubble.
I can see the scar just above its neckline
where once the coal company drilled a test well.
Harsh August light catches every mangy missed spot,
every thin and straggling stalk. The field is embarrassed,
ducks its head to avoid my eyes, a kid at the barber
for the first time.

Looking Glass Prairie

> *"There it lay, a tranquil sea or lake without water, if such a simile be admissible, with the day going down upon it: a few birds wheeling here and there: and solitude and silence reigning paramount around."*
> Charles Dickens, upon visiting the Looking Glass Prairie just east of St. Louis, 1842

We're in the gloaming now,
the air still and replete with the day's doings.
Cottonwoods talk amongst themselves, just the topmost branches
rustling in a breeze we can't feel, like grownups gossiping
over the heads of children. I wish I knew
if they were talking rain—they can see so much further
out across already darkened plains. The moon
keeps trying to foist a streetlight glow off on the prairie,
but it just glances off the big bluestem,
forms an icy crust, even in these dog days.
From the linden a mockingbird chuckles,
whistles the night in over his soft twilight wings.

Roadkill

Fawn, only just past spots, spewing
still-wet bloody foam from its nose
and mouth, maybe warm, I don't know.
Can't bear to notice too much.
Belly already breached, flies
have congregated on the stench,
the spilt raveling of gut.

From the stop sign half a mile away
I saw the wheeling wings, the great settling,
then ungainly upheaval into oncoming traffic.
It's a quiet road, but not that quiet.
I could have turned off, driven south
And done no harm, but no good either.
So I drove on, past it, made a u-turn, put on my flashers.

Walking back, I stretch a stray sock onto my hand,
maybe to breathe through, but mostly to drag that
lost life off to nestle in the ditch full of daylilies.
Safe from being struck again and again by wheels,
safe for an eagle to land on and feast.

Summer Quilt

July, too close and muggy to sleep upstairs.
We're sent to sleep on the screened porch,
low-slung camp cots hovering just above the cool concrete floor.

Tucked under smooth cotton sheets that smelt of the sun,
the quilt was hardly needed, but the rites of summer
must be observed before the grownups will recede.

Just a plain block quilt, thin squares of chambray, houndstooth,
blowsy bandanna paisley, blue Indian batik,
grey and yellow windowpane plaid, nautical stripes.

My favorite showed a bulldog kicking his way across
a field of daisies, clad in a chunky turtleneck fisherman's sweater
like the Clancy Brothers in my mother's rack of albums.

At the time I was sure he belonged to the girl in the green
polka dot dress two squares over. Surely they lived
in the colorful townscape along the quilt's bottom edge,
 n the orange house with the blue door?

I hoped he did not live with the staid Victorian children
in the next square over, trapped in their medallion print,
or with the monochrome couple in toile
too involved with kissing for my eight-year-old self.

Now I think that they live in the squat red and white mushroom houses
on the far quilt edge and will hopscotch their way over gingham,
slide over stripes and pick their way across calico meadows,
holding hands, as soon as I close my eyes.

Carp Quake

After dinner we amble down the pasture,
gathering dew darkening Daddy's pant cuffs.
I dance ahead, eager to display my discovery.

Under the ripe summer moon three massive carp
plunge and veer, their scales rivet bright,
tails threshing through the pond's green field.

A far cry from the placid, dull-as-daylight sunfish,
so stupid I can catch them on my pinky,
flip them out onto the bank in a blue-bottle flash.

These are more like artifacts of another age,
giant plated denizens of the Pleistocene deep
dancing a frenzied foxtrot across our muggy pond.

My father's theory is the heat has brought them up.
Then, as we turn for home, the grass ripples once
beneath us, a rumbling wave of surging earth.
We lurch like drunken sailors, floundering on fluid ground
while the carp ride out the cresting pondswell.

Songs My Mother Taught Me

Whippoorwill, wake robin, black walnut
Sheep sorrel and shaggy mane
Queen Anne's Lace and cottonmouth.

Jimsonweed, persimmon, trillium
Wintercress and sassafras,
Chicory and sycamore.

Whistlepig, mayapple, meadowlark
Copperhead and periwinkle
Pokeberry and Deptford pinks.

Fleabane, tulip tree, teasel
Dewberry and spring beauties,
Dill worms and blue darners.

Redbud, sweetgum, bloodroot
Junebug and autumn olive
Boxelder bugs and mourning cloaks
Cahokia, Piasaw, Peabody Coal.

Late Harvest

Brought outside past midnight by the fierce belling cry of a fox,
I linger at the edge of the deck, October's moon guttering overhead
under a shroud of cirrus, casting its white marble gaze down the valley.

I can hear the muffled roar of our neighbor working late,
fumbling his machinery up and down darkened fields, ratcheting
beans in through great green teeth, throwing up a dusty, halogen lit
halo just visible through the windbreak pines.

The wind smells sharp and tinny, whispering of snow, of sleep.
I turn to go in, catch a billow of breath in the flashlight's frosty beam.
On the driveway verge the vixen's eyes glow cold and green and a drift
of feathers sifts through her teeth. She's up late too, night combining.

Possum Lights

Returning home late in the new moon darkness,
our headlights fan out across the orchard,
forming a dusky cave of light over the apple-strewn drive.

Frequently we see twin fawns feeding on windfall fruit.
They turn in tandem to our lights,
souls shuddering in their skulls behind their frosty, reflective gaze.

Tonight the deer have abandoned their post,
ceding the crab apples to lesser kin.
A plump silvery possum wades into the pooled light,
trailing his naked, reptilian tail in the dust.

We expect the usual possum melodrama:
Blanche DuBois fainting under the lights.
But this possum, perhaps tipsy on too-ripe fruit,
bares his needle teeth in a hiss and comes for us.

Tons of steel surrounding us cannot compete with his cruel grin.
Tired of being typecast as jester, he intends to fix our wagon:
to chew through our headlights and transfix us with his eerie red eyes,
to trap us, breath caught between our teeth, frozen in possum lights.

Ashes and Fat

Lying on my side, birthing ashes from the woodstove,
from the chimney mouth I pull down crackling clinker,
crow colored and sharp as knapped flint, sharp
as the eyeteeth of grandpa's prize sow,
struggling against my arm but too tired to turn,
sink them into me. Just turned twelve,
I'd been judged to have the nimblest fingers
for untangling a knot of piglets,
stoppered up and wedged in sideways.
We exhausted each other, the sow and I,
all squeeze and slip, tangle and twist,
till ten tiny pigs pushed and pulled at her teats,
one stillborn wrapped in a burlap bag and borne away.
I washed up in a bucket, the soft handmade soap
sliding through my fingers. It smelled sharp, stung
a little where the scrub brush bit my skin.
Made with lye leached from last winter's ashes,
the leaf lard from past generations of pig,
caustic cooked to clean with the hulk of hog.

The Dark Season

In our closest neighbor's field winter wheat has come up,
a desperate, violently green blanket.
Further down the road they've left last year's corn stubble
all season, not bothering to plant.
There was no spring fug of "old gold" being spread,
no hot yellow haze of August pollen on the wind.
I'm sure old Norby's plan was to sell up, take his wife
and his farmer's lung to Tucson.
Let a developer try to sprout a crop, grow ticky-tacky
condos on Technicolor lawns.
Now in November the fallow fields lie still
as a plucked chicken, pale, naked and frail.
Even weeds won't pick a fight with that sickly dirt,
alternately poisoned and pushed to produce.
Only tweedy wild turkeys are left to straggle up the drive,
panning for the gold nobody planted.

West with the Night

Behind me the moon came up, a bright
sour lemon slice garnishing the cool blue cup
of a sky salt-spangled with stars.

Ever contrary, I drove
over the fly-over states, the dark
bounding ahead of my headlights,
eager and brisk, bristling with frost.

It was too cold to snow—later
I would learn that as I drove it was colder
here than it was on Mars, but it seemed to me
I was my own planet,
the car swaddled in a muggy atmosphere
of coffee steam from a dented gray-green thermos,
cocooned in the safe known orbit of oldies radio, of white
highway lines and the tail-lights of semis.

Fast as I drove, the moon beat me there, creeping out
over the crown of my car, casting a wan grainy glance
over his shoulder at the day, waiting all eager to tuck him
into the layette colored flannel of morning fog.

Frugality

The wind tastes tinny here on the edge of November.
Skeleton maples wave their arms skyward among stolid, rusty oaks,
pointing out the glowering tar-paper sky.
Last night's storm has brought down the leaves
and the light. Tonight we'll turn back
our clocks, cease to save daylight.
As if it could be hoarded, stockpiled. All that saving
avails us nothing when January ice attacks power pylons,
when snow seals us up tight as pantry canned goods.

Perhaps that light we're saving powers
instead the lightning bug's Morse code missives
afloat on endless summer dusk,
the Perseids showering down August nights,
the aurora's brilliant, chilly flames.
Our lone attempt at frugality, frustrated by
profligate Nature.

Irruption

When he comes, I am in the kitchen, studying shadows
on moon bright snow. The chimney spews smoke to roll wildly,
drunken in the night air, the ghosts of sturdy, Calvinist oaks
set to tumbling like court jesters. They were young once,
when Halley's Comet seared the sky, and still know how to dervish
in the wind. Then he is there, a stern milky mirage
perched on the clothesline. Beak a scimitar, sharp as sunlight,
and eyes that follow beyond thought. My inner rodent quails,
frozen in his ceramic gaze before he turns into the west wind
and is gone, a skirl of smoke adrift across the darkened prairie.

Epiphany

An El Niño year, a winter more likely so far
to spawn tornadoes than a blizzard. Until
this morning when sharp snow skirls in low
over the garden, blows over the last row
of Brussels sprouts, desiccated bones of summer.

Under the willows the pond is a slick black stone
swept clean by a lone crow's wing,
a frozen blade on which to hone the wind.
From the swamp the blows of a woodpecker's ebony beak
echo and ring with cold. A flock of snowbirds swirls, settles,
cloistering the yard as they comb it for any crumb of truth.

Noticing

How
after a rain, the mud at the edge of the drive
loves the wild turkeys, holding their autographs
for days.

How
freshly laid asphalt steams after a sharp
July shower, as do four turkey buzzards in a roadside oak,
their pinions outstretched in worship against the sky.

How
the starlings congregate on the edge of October,
fellowship in the scraggy hedges by the parking lot,
a hidden chorus of sweet whistling kibbitz.

How
the ululating trill of the crane falls with cold rain,
a raft of invisible wings bearing the sky
south for the winter.

Century Farm

White clapboard worn to silver sits
straddling the crest of a dark wave of soil,
sailing a froth of sand atop the dark, implacable earth.
Below us in the trough, hidden now by the spray
off June's green bowsprit runs the river,
the current towards which we are slowly,
inexorably crashing, the hill a wave that reared
past glaciers, has been traveling back
ever since to the depths, slumping
under the weight of us: a century
at least of cowbells and beehives,
of pitchforks and silo staves,
whiskey bottles and baling twine.
Our five generations mere flotsam and jetsam,
derelict cargo borne along on the current of years.
Just detritus to be swept under the keel.
The earth plows itself, slowly turning us all under.

Jessi Peterson grew up roaming the fields and woods of southern Illinois and western Wisconsin, where she learned the singular magic that comes from knowing the names of things, be they animal, vegetable or mineral. She lives in a cordwood cabin she built with husband Dan overlooking the Chippewa River in western Wisconsin. When not working as a children's librarian, she oversees a changing cast of livestock on their farmstead, serves as a poetry reader for literary journal *Barstow and Grand*, and enjoys foraging for wild foods and poems.

www.ingramcontent.com/pod-product-compliance
Lightning Source LLC
LaVergne TN
LVHW041523070426
835507LV00012B/1780